5 Strategies for Successfully AND Profitably Marketing YOUR Business Online!

**Recession Proof YOUR Business
& *DOMINATE <u>YOUR</u> MARKET*
by Turning Your Website Into
An Automatic Marketing &
Lead Generation Machine!**

— by Mike Magana

**www.MarketingByMike.co
909 973-0312**

particular purpose.

Attention Business Owners —
Is Your Website An Automatic Marketing
& Lead Generation Machine?

If you have a business, large or small, you may not be taking advantage of one of the biggest assets you have.

It has the potential to <u>fully</u> automate almost 100% of your marketing, can automatically collect leads, follow-up with those leads [for up to a year], all while pre-selling clients on using your products or services.

And in some cases it can close sales for you...24 hours-a-day, 7 days-a-week, 365 days-a-year.

The best part is it doesn't require you to be at the office. You can be fishing, sleeping, Barbequing with friends, traveling the world, or whatever...it doesn't matter. What matters is, this asset works *even* when you don't...and it doesn't take breaks, vacations, or doesn't ask for raises.

It doesn't need sleep, and it doesn't get sick. It doesn't need days off, and it doesn't have "off" days, <u>AND</u> you *don't* have to pay payroll taxes for it.

It's also *incredibly* loyal... it won't leave you for one of your competitors, when a better offer comes along. It'll be the most affordable, hardest working, most efficient, effective, and most profitable employee you could *ever* 'hire' in your business...bar none.

If you haven't already guessed, what we're talking about is your website. But *not* your average, ordinary website. Nope. We're talking about turning your website into an *automatic marketing* and *lead-generation machine.*

Turning Your Website Into An Automatic Marketing And Lead-Generation Machine...

If you want to turn your website into an automatic marketing and lead-generation machine...it's gonna need a make-over. In fact, it'll need a super-makeover...blue tights, red boots, cape and all.

When your website gets its super-powers, it'll be faster than a speeding bullet, more powerful than a locomotive, and it'll leap tall buildings in a single bound...well...sorta.

Your Pretty Website Sucks!
[cash right out of your pocket]

The *last thing* you need to do is to spend a bunch of money on a "pretty" website that just sits there and does nothing.

You want your website to *automatically* bring you more leads, more sales, and more profits. But what if you *already* have one of those lazy, pretty websites? Armed with the information in this book, and some elbow grease, you can easily change that. How, you ask? By leveraging technology, that's how.

When you do it right, you can *turn your website into an automatic 24/ 7 lead-generation machine*, churning out so many qualified leads, it'll have you grinning so wide, you could eat a banana sideways. ☺

That's EXACTLY why *savvy* business owners leverage the awesome power of Internet. To *fully* **automate [nearly 100%] of their marketing.** It's been done countless times, and there's no reason why you can't do it too.

If you do choose to leverage the power of Internet & set up an automatic marketing and lead-generation system, the return on your investment, can be much larger than anything you've seen in a long, long time.

Listen, I wish I could quote you some numbers and tell you what you can expect, but I can't because...

1) It's ILLEGAL for me to do so (*after all, you could lose money*)
2) Your results will be based on your Internet Marketing and Lead-generation skill-set, as well as how effectively you integrate that skill-set into your current marketing mix, and...

3) You *really* wouldn't believe me if I told you.

So I'm not gonna do it.

What I will say however, is it's an investment that can pay dividends for years (and years) to come. And in today's economy, is a *must* to maximize cash-flow and profitability.

Here Are The 5 Strategies Needed To Recession-Proof Your Business AND Automate Your Marketing:

1) Design or redesign your website to be marketing focused (direct-response), with calls-to-action on *every* page, (remember it's NOT a beauty contest).

2) Leverage technology to turn your site into a non-stop, 24/7, lead-generation machine that *automatically* captures prospect data, and follows-up with *every* lead for at least 90 days   (preferably for 4-6 months).

3) Implement a <u>Proven-buyers List Building System</u>™ (**NOTE**: Studies have shown it's 6 times more expensive to sell to a 1st time customer, than it is to sell to an existing or past customer). *[Source: Marketing Metrics]*

4) Position your website & Google Places listing to rank at the top of Google's Search Results, as well as in the organic search results at Google, Yahoo, Bing, etc.

5) Work with a knowledgeable direct-response marketer to drive traffic to your website. Because what's the point of paying good money to have a website made if no one is ever going to see it, right? [more on this in a minute].

As a busy business owner, even if you only made the time to implement just 2 of the 5 strategies above, you would quickly understand what all the fuss is about online marketing. It's called leverage. When used properly, the Internet is the world's most powerful marketing tool, without equal.

When you harness the power of the Internet and put it to work to automate your marketing, set up Proven-buyer List Building Systems™, and create hands-free lead-generation machines, it's not only possible to dominate your local market, but you can also generate consistent profits that can massively improve your bottom line.

That said, let's take a few minutes and dig a little deeper into each of the 5 strategies mentioned above, so you'll have the best chance of not only surviving [but thriving], when times are tough.

Strategy #1 – Design Or Re-Design Your Website To Be Marketing Focused (*Direct-Response*), With Calls To Action On Every Page...

Before we talk about designing or re-designing your website, let me make an important point: of all the business owners I've worked with...*direct-response marketing* is probably one of the most misunderstood terms in business. Why?

In my experience, it's because most business owners equate direct-response marketing with direct-mail, flyers, postcards [which it is], but there's *much* more to it than that.

Direct-response marketing can take many forms and be done many different ways. But regardless of the marketing strategies & tactics used, in the end the goal is always the same...to get a response. It's simply about getting prospects to take a pre-determined action, or what I like to call your M.W.A [most wanted action].

Your M.W.A.'s can include receiving phone calls, ordering from your website, subscribing to your email newsletter, requesting a FREE guide or whitepaper, or whatever.

But the *real* power, of direct-response marketing is that it aims to get people to respond and take action NOW!

That's the goal...for your prospects to get off the fence and take some sort of *immediate* action. Which, as a business owner, is *exactly* what you need, right?

Think about it for a minute, do you *really* need more tire-kickers in your life?

[I didn't think so!]

What you *need* are prospects. But not just *any* prospects ... you need *qualified* prospects. Prospects who are interested enough in what you have to offer, to take action, to learn more about your offer, to call you, or place an order, *and* do it NOW.

That's what direct-response marketing is all about. And that's why your site needs to be...

A Marketing Focused (Direct-Response) Website...

For internet savvy business owners, a direct-response website is a means to an end. It's simply a vehicle to get your phone ringing, to build a list of qualified prospects, and to sell (hopefully more of) your products or services.

But most business owners don't have the foggiest idea about how to make that happen, not a clue.

Their website is just sitting there in cyberspace, doing nothing. Which is about as effective as having *a billboard on the moon*.

Or worse yet, they've managed to get some visitors coming to it, but don't understand why the phone isn't ringing.

While there can be many reasons, here are some of the most common I've run across...

1) Their website [that was designed by some slick web designer who knows NOTHING about marketing], talks

solely about themselves & their business and how great they are, while *totally neglecting* the wants, needs, and desires of their prospects, and...

2) There's no offer or call-to-action (C.T.A.) anywhere [at all], which in direct-response, is like marketing suicide and is a big, big no-no. Internet experts agree, you should have at least one C.T.A. or call-to-action on *every* page of your website.

3) The visitors coming to their site weren't targeted.

NOTE: A call-to-action (C.T.A.) is simply a strong suggestion to get your prospect to take your desired action. C.T.A.'s can be as simple as '*Buy Now*', or '*Add to Cart*', or can be more benefit oriented like:

'*To learn how we can help you increase your leads, sales, and profits ... Call Us Now @ 704-980-9634*'.

Using C.T.A.'s in your marketing is a simple, yet extremely powerful way to get your prospects to take action. Especially when your lead-generation activities put you in front of a lot of interested, qualified prospects.

The reality that most business owners [and sadly, most web design firms] don't understand is that a website *isn't* a brochure (at least it shouldn't be, if you're interested in *maximizing* profits).

It's a marketing vehicle that should be designed from-the-ground-up to *proactively* generate more leads, more sales, and more profits. It *never, ever* should just sit there!

Strategy #2 – Leverage Today's Technology By Turning Your Website Into An Automatic, Non-Stop, 24/7, Lead-Generation Machine...

Interestingly enough, the one thing that shocks me most about 99.9% of the businesses I work with is this:

The <u>Very</u> Thing That Can Make
A Business Owners' Financial Dreams
Come True, Is The *ONE* Thing Most
Business Owners SUCK AT, BIG-TIME!

Can you guess what it is? No? OK, enough suspense ...

It's Lead-generation.

Yep, lead-generation.

It boggles my mind – you'd think effective, cost efficient lead-generation, would be one of the top priorities of most businesses...but sadly, and mysteriously, it's not.

I'm constantly amazed at the amount of waste that exists in the lead-generation, capture and follow-up processes I see.

And the problem isn't isolated to just a few businesses here and there...it exists *in nearly every business* I deal with.

Did you know mastering the art of lead-generation was *the key* to success in business? Don't believe me? OK, fine, you don't have to, but let me ask you a quick question...

What would happen to your business if you didn't have any leads coming in for let's say...6 months?

Think about it, no leads at all ...
***not even one* ... for 6 LONG MONTHS.**

Right. Doors closed. And case closed. Lead-generation is one of the most critical skill-sets <u>every</u> business *must* master, without exception, if they intend to *stay* in business.

Lead-generation DON'Ts...

The two *most wasteful* lead-generation activities are:

1) Not capturing the contact info of *every* prospect that shows an interest in your products or services, and ...

2) Not *consistently & automatically* following up with your prospects. Studies have shown it takes a *minimum of 7* separate points-of-contact for a potential customer or client to feel comfortable enough to buy from you.

But if you're not capturing your prospects contact information and storing it in a database...how can you follow-up with them, to assess their wants, needs, etc., and educate them about your business, its products or services?

Well it's obvious, if you're not capturing their contact info, you can't follow-up with them. And because you're not automatically following-up with them, you could be leaving a *huge* amount of revenue on the table. *A seriously HUGE amount of revenue* …

Probably 50% or more. No joke, follow-up is THAT powerful.

So the lesson for Strategy #2 [lead-generation] is simple...1) Capture your interested prospects contact details...and 2) Follow-up with them consistently and automatically.

The lead-generation break-down...

Here's what you'll need to create a non-stop, 24/7, automatic marketing and lead-generation machine, that works for you, whether you're fishing, sleeping, or even on vacation:

- ➢ **A Domain Name** (so your prospects can type your web address into their browser and find your site – y*our domain name points to your website*.

- ➢ **A Web Hosting Account** (where your website's pages, images, media, etc. are stored).

- ➢ **A Website** (where you send your prospects/ clients to learn more about your business, etc.).

- ➢ **A Lead-capture Form** (captures your prospects or clients names, email addresses, etc., and saves that info to your online database, the heart of your automated lead-generation system).

> **An Auto-responder** (an *automated* permission-based email follow-up system that seamlessly integrates with your online database).

> **A Database** (to store all captured prospect and or client information).

> **Personalized, Pre-programmed Sales Emails** (Newsletters, sales messages, offers, educational materials, trainings, reports, etc. Your sales messages, promotions, etc., can be written in advance and pre-programmed into your auto-responder to be delivered at whatever intervals you decide).

The Profit-Power Of A Properly Executed Lead-Generation System

Before we wrap up this section on lead-generation...let's talk numbers. Take a minute, and go grab a pen and a calculator. Go ahead, I'll wait. ☺ Got em'? Good, let's get started.

As an example, say over the period of a month, you manage to generate 100 leads from your marketing, which averages out to *only* 3-4 leads a day.

Out of those 100 leads, how many (on average) would end up doing business with you? How many buy your product or service? 10? 20? More? Less? Grab a pen and write that number down here: _____.

Ok, now subtract that number from 100 and write it down here: _____. These are the remaining prospects you need to follow up with.

Now, let's take the remaining leads, and say we implement a strong follow-up program using your shiny-new automatic, lead-generation follow-up system.

What do you think it would mean to your bottom-line if you closed an additional 5% of them? 10%? 20%? Why not take a minute and figure it out? Be conservative or *go big*, the choice is yours.

Here's the formula:

_____ (remaining leads) **X** ____% (follow-up closing percentage) = _____ (follow-up leads closed).

Now take the number follow-up leads closed and write it here ____. Then write what your average sale is worth here $_____ (guess if you have to...or take your annual sales and divide it by the # of customers you generated in that year).

Now take the number of follow-up leads closed and multiply it times your average sale:

_____ (follow-up leads closed) **X** $_____ (average sale) =

$_____ (follow-up profits)

NOTE: It's important to remember...these are profits you *never* would have seen, without implementing an automatic lead capture and follow-up system.

Pretty cool, huh? But here's the coolest part, the additional revenue you just calculated was for 1, 1 month period. Now, take your follow-up profits and multiply them times 12, because there *are* 12 months in the year, right? Right!

$_____ (follow-up profits) **X** 12 (months) =

$_____ (additional annual revenue).

Are you starting to see why savvy business owners, the world-over, are calling the Internet the greatest and most powerful marketing tool in existence?   I hope so.

Strategy #3 – Implement a "Proven-buyers" List Building System™ [VERY powerful for retailers] ...

If you own a brick-and-mortar/ retail business, your most profitable offers will be made to your database of *proven-buyers*, which is very different than your database of leads.

Your proven buyers are repeat-customers, people who have done business with you before. They're prospects, turned customers, turned repeat-customers.

Your repeat customers know you, like you, and trust you, that's why they buy from you again and again. If they didn't know you, like you, and trust you, why would they continue to do business with you?

The truth is, they wouldn't. Now I'm not a big fan of hype. But here's what I [and any business person worth-their-salt] know:

While it's easy to see that generating *qualified* leads can help you stay in business, it's <u>CRITICAL</u> to understand that...

Repeat Customers Can Make You Wealthy!

Let me say that again...

Repeat Customers Can Make You Wealthy!

So Treat Them Like Gold!

If you have repeat customers, you'd better treat them right. They truly hold the-keys-to-the-kingdom. And they know it, but here's the thing...they want to <u>know</u> that *you* know it.

Because the moment they feel like they aren't being appreciated, they're *gone*. So you *have* to go out of your way to show them you value their business *way* more than just a regular one-time customer.

And you'd better, because it's 5X-6X more expensive to bring a new customer through the door, than it is to sell to an existing customer.

Here are a few more facts, you may find interesting:

> The probability of selling to an existing customer is 60-70%: And there's only a 5-20% probability that you will sell to a new prospect. **Source: Marketing Metrics**

> Just a 10% improvement in customer retention [repeat sales], results in a 30% increase in the value of the company: That's absolutely huge, and although effort is involved, the process of implementing a sound customer retention strategy isn't hard. **Source: Bain & Co.**

> A 5% increase in customer retention can increase business profits by 25% to 125%: Read it again if you have to, because those increases again, are huge! **Source: Gartner Group and "Leading on the Edge of Chaos", Emmett C. Murphy and Mark A. Murphy**

If you've been paying attention, you know that repeat customers can make or break your business. So let me ask you, what are you doing to proactively cultivate those relationships?

What are you doing to make sure your repeat customers get what they want? What are you doing to make them feel special, important, appreciated?

Hopefully, you're proactively cultivating repeat customer relationships. If you're not and if you don't have a formal customer retention strategy in place, you need [at the minimum] to *immediately* let your repeat customers know how much you value their business. Thank them. Or make them a special offer.

But, if you *really* want to knock the ball out of the park, increase your cash-flow, and *maximize* your business profits...

Create A *Preferred-Customer Program* For Your Business!

Think about it...who doesn't want to be a preferred-customer? Even by just saying the name, people know *preferred-customers* get treated differently, they're special, they're set-apart from your 'regular' customers [or they should be].

The whole reason to create a *preferred-customer* program in the first place, is because preferred-customers WANT to do MORE business with you. *They want you to send them offers*. They WANT to know about your sales, special offers, discounts, coupons, new product announcements, and closed-to-the-public *preferred-customer* events.

I'd be willing to bet that most of your repeat customers would jump at the chance to become *preferred-customers*. And I think you'd agree, having a *preferred-customer* program would be great for your bottom-line *and* great for your customers…it's a <u>true</u> win-win situation.

People LOVE To Be Treated Like They're Special!

And your preferred customer program, does *exactly* that, makes your customers *feel* special.

Building a *preferred-customer* program is easy. All you need to do to create a **Proven Buyers List Building System ™**.

It may sound complicated, I know, but a **Proven Buyers List Building System ™** is simply a way of creating a database of repeat customers.

And, when it's an *online* database, you can send your *preferred-customer* offers literally at the push of a button.

Setting up a **Proven Buyers List Building System ™** is similar to creating the automated lead-generation system we talked about on Page 6, with one BIG difference…

The people in your automated lead-generation system *aren't* your customers yet…

The people in your *Proven Buyers List Building System ™* are!

So to maximize the profitability of your Proven Buyers List

Building System ™, you want to keep it in its own database, separate from your prospects database. Why?

Because your preferred-customers are '**PROVEN**' buyers, they've already spent money with you, *and* have taken the time to enroll in your *preferred-customer* program, the offers you send to '*preferred-customers'* should <u>ONLY</u> be for *preferred-customer*s.

Your preferred-customer offers will serve you in 2 ways:

1) Your offers will remind preferred-customers how much you value their business and..

2) The special deals, discounts, coupons, closed-door events, etc. will remind them of the benefits of being and remaining one of your preferred-customers.

Here's The Secret To Getting *'Proven Buyers'* **To Sign-Up For Your Preferred-Customer Program** …

Knowing you need to set-up a Preferred-customer program is only half the battle, the other half is getting people to sign up for it. But thankfully you have me in your corner, so implementation will be a piece of cake ☺.

If your business gets a decent amount of foot-traffic, you'll leverage that foot-traffic to get people to sign up for your "Preferred-customer program".

But before we get to that, let me ask you a question:

What's the ONE thing *everyone* who buys something from your business leaves with? The product? Yes. But they also get a … **RECEIPT**.

And as you'll discover next, receipts are the KEY to a profitable 'Preferred-customer program'!

ATTENTION RETAIL BUSINESS OWNERS:
Your Cash Register and Credit Card Receipts
Are *Your Secret Weapon* for Growing Your Business!

In a minute, I'm going to show you how to use your cash register and credit card receipts to set up a *preferred-customer program*, but first let's take a look at an example of what some successful retailers have done.

They took the header info [the header usually has the business name, address, phone, etc.] on their cash register and/ or credit card receipts and put it to work for them by replacing it with the following:

> **We Appreciate Your Business!**
> **For Preferred Customer Discounts**
> **and Coupons Visit:**
> **www.yoursite.com/pc.html**
> **It's FREE!**

That's it. That's all there is to it. Isn't it funny how sometimes the most powerful things are also the simplest? So do yourself a favor and don't discount the power of this simple, yet highly profitable strategy.

If someone knows you, likes you, and trusts you enough to consistently spend money on your products or services, it's *really* a no-brainer for them to sign-up for your *Preferred-customer program*. Again, it's *free* for them and can be an *absolute* Goldmine for you.

Note: You can also put a flyer in their bag, and have your sales staff educate customers about your Preferred-customer Program, etc..

All that said...you'll need to leverage technology to successfully implement a Preferred-customer Program in your business, but it will be well worth it.

Here are the tools you'll need to implement a Preferred-customer Program:

> **A Preferred Customer Sign-up Page** (where your send customers who have made a purchase with you to sign-up for your *preferred-customer program*)

> **A Lead-capture Form** (captures your prospects or clients names, email address, etc., and saves that info to your online database, which is the heart of your system)...

> **An Auto-responder** (an *automated* permission-based email follow-up system that seamlessly integrates with your online database)...

> **A Database** (to store all captured prospect and or client information)...

> **Personalized, Pre-programmed Promotions** (preferred-customer special offers, discounts, coupons, new product announcements, and closed-to-the-public preferred customer events, can be planned AND programmed into your auto-responder in advance)

> **Professionally Designed Coupon(s) and Flyers** (to get customers, with money to spend into your store, by a specific date/ time, so you can better estimate your cash-flow)

For some, setting up a *Preferred-customer Program* can seem complicated, but believe me, the returns from having this powerful system set up in your business, can be amazing.

If you're not technical, or *you don't have the time to set this powerful system up in your business* ... you may want to find someone who can help do it for you.

Your Preferred-Customers Will Be Your BEST AND Most Profitable Customers!

So whether you set it up yourself, or have it done for you…the sooner you get a *Preferred-customer* program up-and-running in your business, the sooner it can work for you growing your company's bottom-line around the clock.

Strategy #4 – Position Your Website & Google Places Listing To Rank At The Top Of Google's Search Results…

If you're finding that the marketing you're used to using isn't as effective anymore, you may want to *carefully read this section of the book*.

As you probably already know, Search Engine Optimization [SEO] is the process of optimizing your website, so the search engines [like Google, Yahoo, Bing, etc.] show your site to the people that are already searching for what you sell.

What you want is for your listing to be among *the first* that someone sees when they go to Google and type in your search term and location. To have the greatest impact on your sales and profits…you want to be on the **1st page** of listings presented to your potential customers or clients.

The reason is simple: *Over 95% of your prospects won't ever go beyond Page 1 in the search results*. And that's truer now more than ever before.

Here's why…

Current trends show more and more of your local prospects are ignoring Pay Per Click [text-based ads on the right side of the page] and are even looking-past organic search results [the normal text-based results], and are OVERWHELMINGLY looking at the "Local Search" results, such as the Google Places listings shown in the below map.

Google Places listings are **1ˢᵗ page** local business results that Google shows normally shows next to a Map. Each local business listing is shown with an orange marker labeled A-G.

<u>NOTE</u>: On 10/27/10 Google changed the way they display & rank 'local' listings, combining the relevance between a business's natural search & Google Places search results.

[Optimizing for BOTH, you can rank MUCH higher in Google's Search Engine for your Website & your Google Places listing]

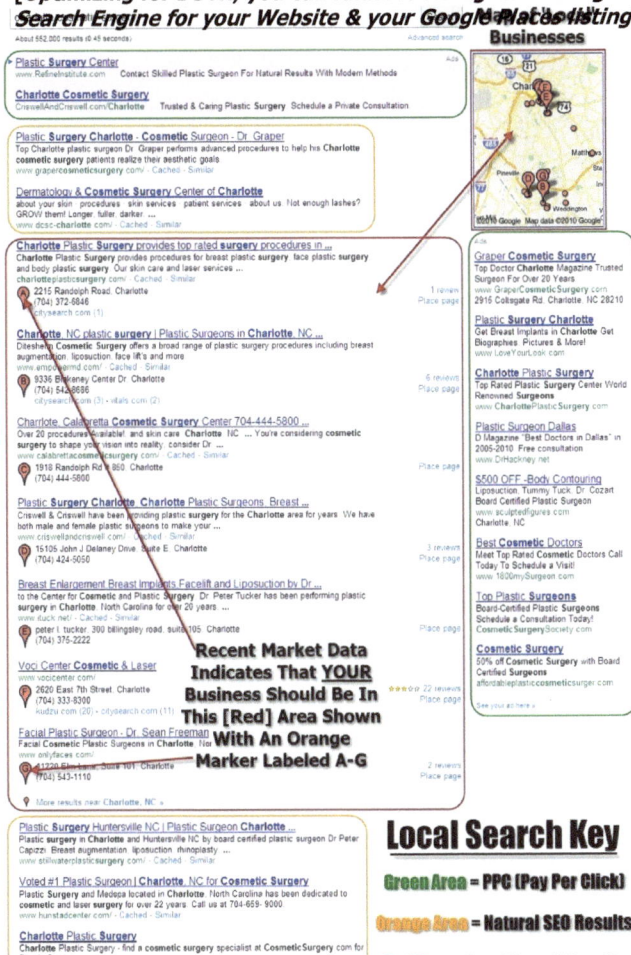

Here Are Some Recent Facts & Trends You May Find

Interesting About 'Local' Internet Usage [Results in Red Box Above]: Sources: com Score, Google, Kesley Group, NPD Group

- ➢ 97% of American internet users use the internet to shop of which 57% characterize their behavior as "shop online, purchase offline" ...
- ➢ 90% of online commercial searches result in offline bricks and mortar purchases ...
- ➢ 82% of local searchers follow up offline via an in-store visit, phone call or purchase ...
- ➢ 74% of internet users perform local searches ...
- ➢ 73% of online activity is related to local content ...

- ➢ 66% of Americans use online local search to locate local businesses ...

- ➢ 61% of local searches result in purchases from local businesses ...

- ➢ 54% of Americans have substituted the internet and local search for phone books ...

- ➢ 35% of all searches are local ...

And did you know that for every dollar consumers in the USA spend online, another 5-6 dollars are going to local offline purchases that are directly influenced by online research.

So to re-cap, here are the two facts I believe have the biggest impact [financially] for the majority of local business owners:

1. **90% of online commercial searches result in local offline purchases...**

2. **61% of all local searches, results in a purchase...**

What these trends and stats mean is that finding businesses locally is becoming *almost exclusively* an internet driven task.

Thanks to local search tools [like Google Places], local businesses are increasingly visible to local customers online.

As a result, the internet is now driving local sales [as well as global e-commerce]. And as consumers continue to move online, their reliance on online tools to perform searches for local information, local businesses, and everything else local, will only continue to grow.

Remember this conversion rate: **61% of local searches result in purchases**. That means that almost 2/3 of customers using local search will go on to buy a local product or service!

When you think about it, a 61% percent local search conversion rate makes perfect sense. Do you know why it makes perfect sense? Let me tell you why …

It's because most people aren't going to look for a local restaurant, plumber, accountant, or any other local business for that matter, *unless they plan on using it*. Now, or in the near future.

When people search for a local seller, they are more than likely motivated to buy.

So here's the question you [*as the owner of a small business*] need to answer …

When <u>Local</u> Prospects Search For What *YOU* Sell...

Do They Find You?

Don't know? See for yourself … go to **www.google.com** and type in something you think a potential customer of yours may be looking for and hit enter… go ahead, I'll be here when you get back.

[What are you still doing here? Seriously, do yourself a favor, and go do that search now!]

So let me ask you, did your business come up in the Google's Local Search Results [in spots A-G] for the keywords you entered? *If your site doesn't show up in the Local Results on Page 1 of Google then …*

Your Local Customers *Won't* Find <u>YOUR</u> Business!

But guess who they <u>WILL</u> find? Yep, you guessed it...

Local Consumers <u>WILL</u> Find *Every-One* of Your Competitors!

... who rank on page 1 in Google's local search listings.

What's worse, those competitors are taking business that could be *your* business, and they're making profits that could be *your* profits, profits that could be dropping straight into *your* bank account.

The value of ranking on page 1 is 3 fold ...

➢ First, it gets your phone ringing and brings in more customers [which is the whole point of marketing online].

➢ Second, it allows you to establish a sequence of ongoing communication, build rapport with these customers, and positions your business in a way that lets prospects become familiar with you, your business, and your offers.

➢ Third, Local SEO not only puts you in front of potential customers, but in many cases, it puts your business *directly in front of people that have already made the decision to buy* [AND who are ready to pull the trigger].

Think about it for a minute...if I'm typing "*charlotte cosmetic dentist*" into Google, it's probably not just because I'm browsing to see who's out there, it's most likely because I'm looking for a dentist that can help solve my cosmetic dentistry problem, right? EXACTLY!

If a local consumer searches for "*charlotte cosmetic dentist*" and a dental practice has their local listing & website optimized properly, there's a very good chance it will appear prominently in Google's new combined local search listings.

As an example, here's a search I did in Google for the term "sedation dentistry":

NOTE: See map image on page 24...

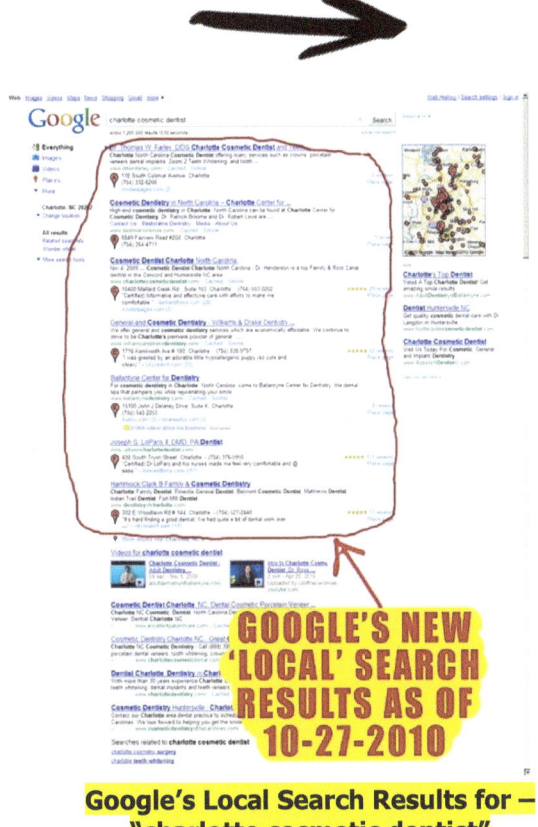

Google's Local Search Results for – "charlotte cosmetic dentist"

The image above is how Google now shows the top 7 local results. [Google ranks these results by relevance from A-G with an orange balloon like this:] In my search for **"charlotte cosmetic dentist"**, Google returns results based on my search term and location, all based on my computers I.P. address.

Without getting too technical, your I.P. address is like your home address, in that it tells [Google] what city you're in, and shows local business search results based on that location.

Ideally, a local consumer will gather dental related information from the main website of the dentist or practice near them, and be influenced to get more information and/ or seek out their services.

The goal here is to shorten the consumer's path from searching and researching to making a purchase.

Overwhelming 'Local' Search Marketing Data <u>PROVES</u> "Local" Search is Where The Money is At...

Did you know that a study done *by The Kelsey Group and ConStat*, showed **74% of U.S. households** now use the Internet when shopping locally for products and services? It's true. That's **74% of U.S. households!**

And even more evidence of this growing trend in local search is presented in *The Kelsey Group's Annual Forecast*, which shows that local [traditional] advertising is shrinking. Going from $155.3 billion in 2008 to an estimated $144.4 billion in 2013.

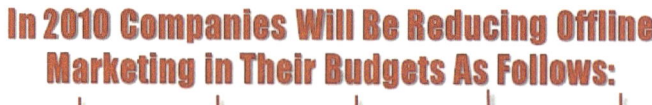

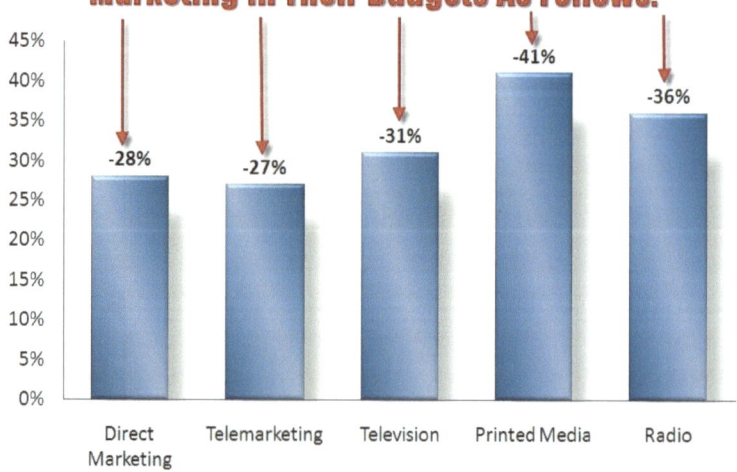

What this means is approximately $11 billion that would normally have been spent on traditional local media (*newspapers, Yellow Pages, direct mail coupons, etc.*) will shift to local search, social networks; mobile and similar digital media spends.

"We Are Seeing A Shift As The Overall Local Ad Media Pie Shrinks Over The Next Five Years."

– Michael Boland, Senior Analyst
The Kelsey Group

So, in light of the mountain of evidence, facts, and statistics presented over the last few pages, I think you'd agree that this fast growing "Local SEO" trend can no longer be ignored.

The bottom line is this...

➢ Local search is here to stay.

➢ It's a trend that [when leveraged properly], can significantly fuel the growth of your local business.

➢ It can open the doors to every customer or client located within the area you service at little or no cost.

Your Clients Are Waiting For You At The Local Search Engines, But Are They Going to Find You There?

Here's The Good, The Bad, And the Ugly of Local Search:

The Good: Your clients will find your business, when your local Google listing consistently appears Google's Local Search Results for your top keywords.

The Bad: *Your clients will find YOUR COMPETITION* when their local Google listing *consistently* appears in the Local Results for your keywords, and *your listing doesn't*.

The Ugly: Your competitors are legally stealing business that could be *your business*, and they're making profits that could be *your profits*, profits that could be dropping straight into *your back account*!

Listen, someone's got to be real with you and tell you the hard truth, so it may as well be me…

If You're NOT Ranking At the Top of The 'Local Results', You Could Potentially Be Losing Multiple-Thousands Of Dollars A Month In Profits…Or More!

Strategy #5 – Hire or Consult With A Top-Notch Marketer [To Be Effective, You Want A Marketer Who Eats, Sleeps, and Breathes Marketing]…

The only way to be sure you *crush your competition* and get your local Google listing consistently appearing in the Local Results for your top keywords is to work with someone who knows what they're doing.

As you know, online marketing is a full-time job. It's *not* something you learn by tinkering around for a few hours here and there. That's why it's *critical* you work with someone who knows *exactly* how to take your local business and market it properly online.

As I See It, You Have 3 Options…

OPTION #1 –

> ➢ Spend hours and hours trying to figure this stuff out on your own.

> ➢ Wasting money in the process, if you happen to mess something up.

> ➢ Worse, the amount of time you'll have wasted if you do happen to mess something up. This is time you'll *never* get back.

> ➢ Deal with the stress of trial and error.

- ➤ Do your own keyword research [and hope you're doing it correctly].

- ➤ Submit and properly optimize your own Google Places Listing.

- ➤ Cross your fingers hoping all of your hard work pays off.

OPTION #2 –

- ➤ Do nothing.

- ➤ Keep doing what you've always been doing.

- ➤ **"If you keep doing what you've always done, you'll keep on getting what you've always got"**

- ➤ Let your competitors *legally* steal business from you.

- ➤ Willingly give up the profits that could be dropping straight to your bottom line.

– OR –

OPTION #3 –

Hire My Company To Do Everything For You & Let Us *Turn Your Business Into A Market Leader*!

Instead of you having to try and figure out what's hype, what's not, where to start, how to scale it, how to track it, and how to analyze it – My team and I do it all for you.

We've been in the industry for more than a dozen years and have been successfully using Google Local Listings [Now Google Places] since before it was "cool."

When you hire my team and I, we become your online marketing partners. Which means we are constantly increasing your online presence. The result is an increase in exposure that can drive more leads, more sales, and more profits into your business.

Why Should You Choose Us
Over Anyone Else?

Listen, I'd never bad mouth another company to try and get my way, but the fact is that *most* "Internet marketing" shops are just web designers who changed their titles a couple years ago.

I don't just dabble in "a little online promotion" for you. My team and I will *shut down YOUR competition* by dominating the conversation taking place online in your local industry. When customers search online for what you provide, you'll be there in dominant fashion.

What Do We Do For You?

The simplest way to explain it is that we make your company visible in an attractive way in every spot where people are looking online locally for services like yours.

This involves getting you top rankings in Google's Local Listings *and* Google's regular search engine listings. We take your local business listing information and submit it everywhere that's relevant and important to get you top listings.

In other words, we put your business smack-dab-in-the-middle of the conversation happening in your local market.

Here's a look at each task we can perform for you...

➢ Design or re-design your website to be both marketing focused & SEO friendly, with calls to action on every page, compelling prospects towards your *most wanted action*. **[see page 6]**

➢ Leverage today's powerful technology and turn your website into an automatic, 24/7, lead-generation machine that collects leads and follows up with them, even if you're sleeping, on vacation, or spending time with family. **[see page 10]**

➢ Implement a "Proven-buyers" List Building System™ – So you can make special offers to *proven* buyers. **[see page 12]**

➢ Using our specialized knowledge about both Local Search Engine Optimization, We Position your website & Google Places listings to rank at the very top of Google's Search Results. **[see page 27]**

What Kind of Results Can You Expect?

First, *by law*, I have to say that we <u>cannot</u> guarantee anything because we don't physically control the people or the third party platforms we advertise on. However, should things proceed without any rare, crazy, or unforeseen issues **you will experience a gradual and lasting increase in new customers**.

Physically, you will be able to start seeing your company mentioned in more and more places online. Until eventually your company is front and center in just about every place where your topic is being talked about locally.

In short, **you will become the market leader through a dominant amount of online exposure** and competitors will *grimace* when they hear your name.

How Much Is This Going to Cost?

You should be more concerned with how much you'll make, because if I show you a way to bring in more than $10,000 per month in new customers, you wouldn't even care that it cost $5,000 per month? You would do whatever it takes to get that money because you would be doubling your investment or more.

Now I'm not saying I can bring you $10k per month or even that my service costs $5,000. In fact, **it's only** half **that price** and **we've made others A LOT more than $10,000**, but we've made some less too.

I wish I could guarantee you a specific number because that would help me sell a lot more accounts, but the fact is that it's illegal for me to do so and impossible to predict. **What I can stand on though is our past performances.**

I'm truly proud of what I do for small business owners like you and I wouldn't do anything else even if it paid more money. I love what I do and I'm addicted to it. Which is why **I'm the only guy in town that you should hire**, because I guarantee you no one will go farther and give you more because no one loves this more than I do.

I Can Only Accept One Client Per Industry, Per City

However, the problem is my methods don't work for two businesses doing the same thing in the same city. **I can only create ONE market leader**, there is no such thing as two market leaders.

I never know who is serious about building their business or not so unfortunately you're not the only one who has received this letter.

It is our policy to not accept more than one client per industry per city.

First of all because I just think that's unethical. It would be like selling weapons to *both sides* in a war.

Second because our strategies are so strong that we just can't perform them for two people doing the same thing in the same city.

We Make Market Leaders...

And last time I checked that's not a title that two people can hold. There aren't two #1 positions in Google and no one goes to two dentist offices at the same time.

This is why it's very important for you to *call us immediately* if you're interested. Our services are first come first serve and if one of your local competitors has called us first, then I'm sorry, but it's too late.

And when you do call, be sure to ask about our "**California 2-Fer**" Local Listings Package, where you can get 6 months of Platinum Local SEO service for the price of 3, when you pay up front.

Online marketing is a full time job. It's not something you learn in a few hours. So it's important to work with someone who knows *exactly* how to take your local offline business and market it properly online.

Putting it all together…

As a fellow business owner, my hope is that you've learned something from this guide that can help you grow your business and you profits.

But more importantly, I want you get a taste of the *freedom* that automation [by leveraging internet technology] can bring into your life AND business.

Because we all know…

Business Automation = Time Freedom

More time for *you*. More time to market your business, more time to spend selling to highly-qualified leads, and more time to spend with friends and family.

Time…it's the one thing we can *never* get back, and once you spend it, it's gone *forever*. So why not leverage technology to take back some of your time and stop spending the majority of it working?

In this guide, I've laid out a solid plan to help you create more sales, more profits, and more time freedom, by leveraging the Internet.

When you leverage the power of internet properly, you'll *turn your website into an automatic marketing and lead-generation machine*…

A Machine That Works For You 24/7, Whether You're Fishing, Sleeping, Or Spending Time With Family!

Someone once said that knowing is half the battle (I think it was G.I. Joe)...the other half is the doing...the implementation...which isn't always easy, especially if that something is new or outside of your skill-set.

If that's the case, and if you've never implemented an integrated (offline/ online) marketing system before...you may want to consider outsourcing it to a Managed Marketing Company that does this star-trek techie stuff full-time.

You know...

The *geeks and dorks* you made fun of in high-school. ☺ And if you need help, give us a call **@ 909 973-0312** *this is what we do.*

As always, I wish you much success!

Take care and God bless,

Mike Magana

Mike Magana, Founder
www.MarketingByMike.co

P.S. – Want to be YOUR industries market leader...but ***don't know where to start?*** Consider asking about our "**California 2-Fer**" Local Listings Package, where you can get 6 months of Platinum Local SEO service for the price of 4, when you pay up front.

HERE'S WHAT
TO Do NEXT ...

Request Our Proprietary Website Analysis & Profit Discovery Marketing Evaluation Now, By Visiting:

www.MarketingByMike.co
(** A $250.00 Value! **)

Here's What To Do Next…

Step 1) Request Your Proprietary Website Analysis & Profit Discovery Marketing Evaluation Now by Visiting:

www.MarketingByMike.co

Step 2) Contact Mike Magana @ **909 973-0312** to arrange a time to go over your Analysis and Marketing Evaluation.

When *you call me*, we'll decide on a time to discuss *exactly* how (and if) I can help you and what your wants and needs are for your business. The initial meeting is always done on the phone and lasts usually no longer than 30 Minutes.

After the initial meeting, if you're local, we'll meet face to face. I am in the Diamond Bar, CA area. If you're not local, we can discuss everything via phone/ email/ Skype/ etc.

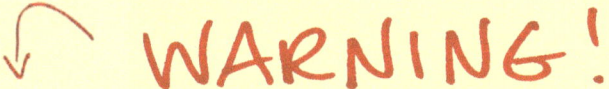 **WARNING!**

- Not everyone will qualify to work one on one with me…
- If the numbers don't add up, then I won't take you on as a client. If your customer dollar value is small, then you will be wasting your money. No sense in you spending hundreds of dollars a month on marketing if you are selling a $2 widget and only sell 50 of them a month. Make sense?…
- Due to the nature of what I do, I can only work with one business owner per market in any city…

- So if you sit around and don't take action as soon as you are done reading this free report, you are risking the opportunity to work one on one with a marketing expert and you will be missing out on a ton of business…
- Instead, your competitor will be raking in the money. Money that could be yours…

Don't Forget These Potentially Profitable Statistics …

- 90% of online commercial searches results in local offline purchases.
- 61% of all local searches results in a transaction.

So Ask Yourself…

"Is This An Opportunity I'm Willing To Pass Up"?

And remember…

"When <u>LOCAL</u> Consumers Search For What You Sell, Will They Find You? OR …

WILL THEY <u>ONLY</u> FIND <u>YOUR</u> COMPETITORS?

Request Your Proprietary Website Analysis & Profit Discovery Marketing Evaluation Now:

www.MarketingByMike.co

Respectfully and profitably yours,

Mike Magana, Founder
www.MarketingByMike.co
909 973-0312